A third helpi

PETER HARVEY'S SHEFFIELD

MANY PEOPLE have asked me : 'Is there going to be another Peter Harvey's Sheffield?' The answer is, yes. This is it. As before, it is a pictorial mixture of city centre and suburbs. All but a few of the pictures are from old picture postcards. Most of them were taken in the Edwardian era, some were taken in the 1920s, one in the 1940s, and at least three are pre-1900.

The picture on the front cover shows Angel Street and from the number of people standing about — many of them on the road — my guess is that it was taken on a Saturday. It would not be advisable to stand about in the middle of Angel Street on a Saturday nowadays.

The picture on this page shows the Town Hall illuminated for the coronation of King George V in 1911. The words 'Long may they reign' can just be made out on the front of the building above the illuminated tram.

I know from the reactions I have had that many of the two previous books were sent to people who used to live in Sheffield and now live elsewhere, in such far-flung outposts as Australia and Hounslow.

If this book also finds its way to emigré Sheffielders, wherever they are, I hope that it will stir some happy memories for them.

The old picture postcard publishers were not in business as social historians. They simply took photographs that they thought people would buy, although the commercial potential of a photograph of one very small street must have been limited. But the cards they published are recognised now as a valuable record of how the city used to look.

The pictures they took are not taken any more. Nobody has published a picture postcard, for example, of Bomber Graham. The old timers would have done. Nobody issued a card showing the Manpower Services Commission HQ being built, the Royal Hallamshire Hospital being opened, the Sheffield Marathon, a university rag parade, the City Clopper, the Bendibus, the first High Speed Train Service in Sheffield, or any one of a hundred other subjects that the old time photographers would have pounced on.

This means that seventy years from now people living in Sheffield will not be able to look back on the 1960s, 70s and 80s as fully or as easily as we can look back on the Edwardian era.

If this book is a tribute to anybody it is to the old photographers who searched all over the city and the surrounding areas for subjects, often showing flair and imagination, and more often than not coming back with some excellent pictures.

First published in 1986 by Sheaf Publishing Ltd,
100 Wellington Street, Sheffield S1 4HX
© Text: Peter Harvey; Design: Sheaf Publishing. ISBN 1 85048 000 1

People who enjoy statistics may like to know that Sheffield's war memorial in Barker's Pool, seen here at its unveiling ceremony on 28 October, 1925, consists of a hollow steel mast which is 108 feet long and weighs ten tons. This explains why, when it arrived in Sheffield from Hull, where it was made, moving it from The Wicker Goods Yard to Barker's Pool took one and a half hours. To avoid disrupting daytime traffic the journey was made at midnight on 14 August, 1925.

The memorial was unveiled by Lieutenant General Sir Charles Harington, GOC Northern Command, and the first wreath was laid by the Lady Mayoress, Mrs A. J. Bailey.

Some of the shops on the other side of the road, on what is now the frontage of Cole Brothers' store, appear to have taken the precaution of nailing boards across their ground floor windows to prevent any mishap. The upstairs windows, as always on such occasions, are wide open and in full use as vantage points. There are even two agile individuals leaning quite a long way out of upper floor windows on Cambridge Street, getting a slightly horizontal view of the ceremony.

War memorial, Barker's Pool, 1913

People who enjoy coincidences may like to know that the statue of King Edward VII in Fitzalan Square, seen opposite, was also unveiled on 28 October, but in 1913. It seems that 28 October is a propitious day for unveiling ceremonies in Sheffield.

The Fitzalan Square picture was taken about 1913, and I am slightly puzzled by the small group of men standing to the left of the statue. They look a bit like members of the environmental projects sub-committee on their annual visit of inspection.

If the Fargate photograph, taken much later, shows anything at all, it shows how daring we all used to be waiting for trams in the middle of the road, protected by nothing more than a white line.

Fargate, around 1950

WIDENING of HIGH STREET.
FOSTERS' HUGE SALE
Previous to Extensive Alterations.
GREAT REDUCTIONS,
In All Departments.
SALE THIS DAY.

W. FOSTER & SON

OLD HIGH STREET. S.P.C. 441.

The widening of High Street was a long-running saga of late Victorian Sheffield. It took 20 years to get a plan agreed and the work done and in the process a great many heated words were exchanged. The first plan was put forward in 1875. It ran into stiff opposition and was dropped. In the 1880s several more plans emerged and were hotly debated before they too were dropped. In 1891 the Town Council decided that it would give no further consideration to any plan for widening High Street. In 1892, the Mayor, Ald Joseph Gamble, submitted another widening plan, and the council turned him down. Two months later, a special committee called The High Street Committee was appointed and, after due consideration, they proposed a £¼ million scheme for widening the street to 80 feet. This was adopted by the council, but only after three hostile amendments had been defeated.

Before the work started, some unknown photographer, no doubt thinking to himself that after 20 years of argument there had to be a picture in it somewhere, took the photograph opposite, showing a horse bus passing the end of York Street, and Foster and Son's shop in the process of holding a sale before the building was demolished.

The building to the left, now the National Westminster Bank, is substantially the same today, but the properties on the opposite corner of York Street were later demolished to make way for what was first called Kemsley House, and is now a group of shops and offices.

Councillor Arnold Muir Wilson, a famous old Sheffield solicitor, was once coming out of a hearing in a Lancashire town when he saw a man with an outfit along the side of which were the words: 'Scissor Grinder — Sheffield'. Doubting the man's credentials, Coun Muir Wilson approached him and asked: 'Are you from Sheffield?'

'Oh yes,' said the man.

'Do you know Snig Hill?' asked the councillor.

'No,' said the man, 'But I know his brother, Charley.'

I don't know how true the story is, but judging by this picture of old Snig Hill, it would be easy to understand someone being unwilling to admit that he knew it. Despite some old advertisements for Guinea Gold Cigarettes, Midnight Flake and Ogden's Fruit and Honey Tobacco (plus an old-style barber's pole), the hill has a decidedly decrepit look about it. I suspect these buildings were also awaiting demolition.

Old Snig Hill. Sheffield. JWM

Snig Hill in the 1890s

The small group of ladies standing outside Wyming Brook Farm seem to be earnestly debating among themselves whether or not to pop in for a buttered scone and a pot of tea. The one with her back to the camera appears to be fiddling about in her pocket, as if checking to see that she can cover the cost of a scone. If not, it might just have to be tea. The children have evidently already made up their minds that a spot of refreshment is a good idea. Since they were not paying, it would not be a difficult decision for them to make. There remains an air of indecision around the adults. Did they, or didn't they? We shall never know.

The thing I have always wondered about the old causeway to Stanage Pole is why, when the paths I make start to crumble after about 18 months, and need replacing after two years, this one, allegedly put down by the Romans in the middle of nowhere, lasted for so long. They had their heads screwed on, did the Romans. Note that they did not waste time and material paving the whole width of the road. They only paved the bit where the wheels ran.

One of the chaps outside Rivelin Bridge Post Office is having a lean, or loll, against the post office wall. Quite a lot of people used to loll when they had their photographs taken in the old days.

Stanage Pole

I hesitate to say anything at all about Upper Cut Mill in Rivelin Valley other than to say that it was a mill and it was located in the Rivelin Valley. There are a great many experts on mills in and around Sheffield and I am not one of them.

My recollections of the Rivelin Valley as a beauty spot are unfortunately coloured by the fact that I was taken there as a youngster by a friend of mine and his mother. It was a bitterly cold day, slightly misty and with a faint drizzle. We paddled, chased about a bit, ate sandwiches, then came home. I left feeling cold and dismal and with the distinct impression that the Rivelin Valley as a fun place was enormously over-rated.

For years after that I never went near the place.

The Norfolk Arms Hotel has a spick and span look about it. There seem to be two galvanised buckets hanging on the front wall which I presume are there to give the horses something to drink in the absence of a horse trough. It's a very thoughtful provision, but replenishing the buckets must have been a bit of a chore for somebody. I bet they had to be refilled every 20 minutes on a busy day.

Norfolk Arms, Rivelin Valley

Glen Mount, Rivelin

The caption says 'Glen Mount, Rivelin', but there is a strong suggestion of the English seaside about this establishment with its whitewashed offers of hot water, sweets, mineral waters and 'all kinds chocolates'. The only thing missing is 'Pots of tea for the sands'.

There is another whitewashed sign on the front of the building which has been rubbed out, but is still faintly legible. It says, or it said: 'Herb beer'. I wonder why it was rubbed out. There are two possibilities. It could be that the herb beer was so popular that the proprietors quickly ran out of stock. Or it might be that the herb beer was so unpopular the previous season that they were left with 20 gallons of the stuff and having spent all winter drinking it themselves, they have decided not to stock it any more.

On the day the Ladybower Inn was photographed, there was a fine collection of vehicles in the inn yard. I make it 12. But there isn't a single horse to be seen anywhere. They have probably been led off somewhere in the nether regions for refreshments of their own in preparation for the long haul back to Sheffield.

This picture proves what I said on the previous page about the two buckets outside the Norfolk Arms Hotel. If this many carriages had arrived at one time outside the Norfolk Arms there would have been something of a stampede for the two buckets. It's fortunate this lot went to the Ladybower instead.

Ladybower Inn

Abbeydale Road, Sheffield. No. 2795.

Abbeydale Road, pictured here in the early 1920s, is not exactly thronged with traffic. There are two motor cars and one cyclist (who either has a puncture, or is fed up with pedalling). Nowadays, there are so many cars it takes half a lifetime just to cross from one side to the other.

Carterknowle Road, photographed earlier in the century, has even less traffic, and not much in the way of humanity, although there are two little girls standing on the right hand pavement, watching the photographer with little-girlish suspicion.

(The thing in the air over the fifth house up on the left hand side is not a Bleriot monoplane. It is a cross made by the person who sent the card to show where his house is).

Totley Rise, now a dual carriageway, was a placid little country road when Gertie and Mabel sent their best wishes for Christmas to Lizzie on the back of this card.

Here then are three photographs showing Abbeydale Road, Carterknowle Road and Totley Rise, with only two motor cars and one walking cyclist between the three of them. Today, it would be necessary to get up at 5am on Christmas morning to take three similar pictures with as little traffic on them.

Carterknowle Road

Totley Rise

This is a quartet of side roads.

Herschell Road, off Abbeydale Road at Highfield, looks as if it was photographed on a very hot day. Both the shopkeeper and the man with a child on the left hand side of the road, are in their shirt sleeves, and the sun blinds are out. Apart from that there is a glare about the picture and a generally indolent atmosphere. The shop on the left hand corner is Swan's Grocery Store. The shop on the other corner is impossible to identify. It says W. White on the blind, but he may not be the shopkeeper, he may be the man who made the blind.

Beeton Road, viewed here from the entrance to Meersbrook Park, looking towards Chesterfield Road, is totally deserted. There isn't even anybody peeking out from behind one of the curtains. The only sign of life is that the park gate has been left open, and it was probably the photographer who did that.

Perhaps the summer sales were on and everybody was in town.

Beeton Road

It seems to be delivery time at Rutland Park, but it is difficult to see what is being delivered. The young man doing the delivering has two crates so it might be spa water. On the other hand it might be the first of the new season's Beaujolais. The lady who sent the card (to a friend at Highgate, London) seems to have been disappointed that she was not on the picture. 'We were obviously spring cleaning when it was taken!' she says.

Here, at Ashland Road, Nether Edge, is another example of lolling by somebody who is having his photograph taken. The young lad on the left-hand pavement is not quite tall enough to loll with any real flare, but he obviously has the makings of a good loller if he perseveres.

My wife and I spent our early married life in a flat which looked up Ashland Road so we became quite familiar with this view.

Ashland Road

Mr Marcus Manton, of Sheffield, became well-known throughout the country as an aviator in the early days of the century. On Whit Tuesday, 1914, about 8,000 people saw him give a flying demonstration at Redmires and were so enthusiastic when he landed that they damaged his plane in the rush.

This photograph of him was taken at Barnsley, in July, 1914, a day when, according to the message on the card, he looped the loop. He was 19 years old at the time.

Skid Skinner's feats were more down to earth. He was a Sheffield speedway rider. In February, 1930, a wall of death was built in the two shilling enclosure at Owlerton track and Clem Beckett and Skid Skinner rode on it every night for the following month.

Frankly, I would have thought it was difficult enough riding round the wall of death without taking your hands off the handlebars as Mr Skinner is doing, below.

Mr Marcus Manton, aviator

Mr Skid Skinner, speedway rider

George Littlewood, of Attercliffe, was a sportsman of a different kind. He was the champion long distance runner and walker of the world. At Madison Square Gardens, New York, in December 1888, he created a world record in a six days' 'go as you please' race, by covering 623 miles and 1,320 yards in the allotted time. In 1882, he walked 200 miles in 40 hours 40 minutes, and 400 miles in 96 hours 30 minutes. When he died in 1912, at the age of 52, one obituarist described him as an athlete of remarkable powers of endurance who was renowned throughout the world.

In the early years of this century rifle shooting enjoyed huge popularity for a time and ranges sprouted up all over the place. (The amphitheatre at Graves Park started out as a rifle range).

Sprouted up is an apt metaphor for this particular range, at Oughtibridge. It is in the middle of a field of vegetables.

The flag on top of the ridge is to let everybody know that shooting is in progress and to deter anybody who feels inclined to wander across the range to pick a couple of cabbages.

Rifle Range, Oughtibridge

George Littlewood.

Mr George Littlewood, athlete

The old Norton post office is seen here during one of its slack periods, and very peaceful it looks too. The two young ladies outside, one sitting on a rain barrel are probably nothing whatever to do with the post office. I know for a fact that the man who took the picture often used to take his children with him when he went out with his camera. This might be them.

It is always infuriating to come across an old postcard with a caption that says it shows 'A bit of old Somewhere-or-Other' without any indication of which particular 'bit' is shown. Fortunately, this bit of old Norton has a street nameplate on it — Norton Lees Lane.

Judging from the paving stones leaning up against the cottage front, the picture was taken at a time when the pavements were being re-done.

The Lodge at Bole Hill, Norton, stands at the entrance to what was then private property, but later became Graves Park. Students of old gas lamps will delight in the specimen to the right.

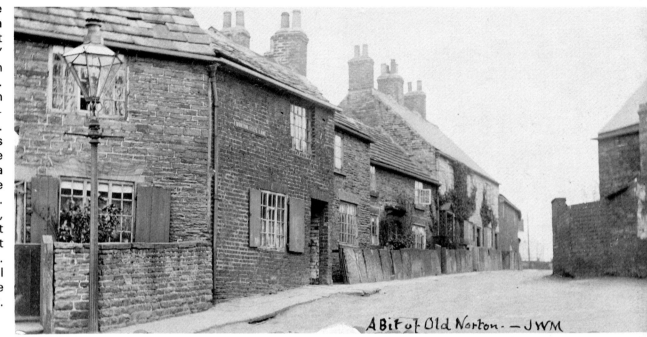

A Bit of Old Norton. — JWM

Lodge, Bolehill, Norton

It is a long time since this many horses were seen on a Sheffield street. The occasion is the William Stones Ltd Cannon Brewery Horse Parade which took place on 14 July, 1913, with everybody lined up on Rutland Road ready for the off. The gentleman in the white jacket with his back to the camera looks like the parade marshal, making sure that everything is as it should be before he gives the order 'Waggons roll!' When the parade concluded and everybody agreed what a fine turn-out it had been, well worth all the hard work, and so on, I bet they were all ready for a drink. I bet they all had one, too.

The smaller rigs here are both milk carts, one belonging to Mr L. Cotterill, of Little Matlock, the other to Tomlinson and Co, of Broomhill Dairy, Glossop Road (on the side of whose cart is a sign saying that in addition to milk they are also suppliers of pure Devonshire clotted cream, cream cheese and Stilton).

Tomlinson's milk cart

Blind School, Manchester Road

Sheffield School for Blind Children, Manchester Road, came about through the generosity of a Victorian benefactor, Mr Daniel Holy. When Mr Holy died in 1870 he left £26,000 for the upkeep of a blind school so long as money could be found from other sources to build it. Money for the building, which cost £15,000, was raised by a public appeal, and the school, set in two acres of land which was laid out as a play area, was opened by Mr Samuel Roberts JP on 24 September, 1879. During the last 20 years there has been much talk of replacing it with a new school, but so far it has amounted to nothing more than talk, and the 104-year-old building is still in use.

There was obviously a crisis of some sort when the ladies on the right were photographed in Southgrove Road. They are all maids from nearby houses and they are in the process of fetching water from a horse-drawn Corporation water cart. I am not sure why this was necessary, but since it is obviously winter, and very cold, my guess is that there was a burst main somewhere in the area.

They are using a variety of containers, among which is a watering can, but considering the circumstances, they look remarkably cheerful.

Unlike most of the pictures in this book, the water cart is not from a picture postcard. It is one half of a stereoscope card which I think was the work of Mr Jasper Redfern, the well known pioneer of photography and cinema in Sheffield.

Southgrove Road

A gaggle of groups.

The footballers are members of St Barnabas, Highfield, Boys' Brigade FC and the gentleman standing second from left is the Rev John St Leger Blakeney, who was vicar of St Barnabas' Church up to 1925, and was interested in all outdoor sports, especially cycling, cricket and football.

The nurses, top left, are from the old Royal Hospital, West Street, and this is how they looked on the night of 29 December, 1910, when they toured the wards with a Christmas entertainment for their patients. Seven are dressed as suffragettes, one as a police sergeant.

The Dannemora Band was an institution in Sheffield. In the days before football grounds had sound systems, and team changes had to be chalked on a board and carried round the ground by a ball boy, they did not have canned music. The Dannemora Band used to play selections before the kick-off and at half time.

For years I thought, mistakenly, that Dannemora was a place in Ireland (perhaps because it sounds like a perverse Gaelic conjunction of Danny Boy and Begorrah). In fact it is a place in Sweden famous for its iron ore. When Seebohm and Dieckstahl set up a works in Sheffield they named it the Dannemora Works, and this was the works band. The firm later became better known as Arthur Balfour and Co Ltd, but the works kept its name and so did the band.

St Barnabas Boys' Brigade FC

Dannemora Band

This, I am assured, is the Salvation Army Concertina Band as portrayed in the early days of this century by a photographer at Darnall.

If his hat and his Goodies waistcoat are anything to go by, the gentleman seated far left represents John Bull, and the gent seated far right, with a different hat and striped trousers, is Uncle Sam.

The chap in the middle, in the check suit, has the look of a Scottish gillie, but after that it's every man for himself in a welter of false beards and shiny toppers.

It is not clear if the two ladies on either side of the gillie are tambourine players, money collectors, or just in attendance to lend moral support.

I can't help wondering what a band consisting of 14 concertinas, two drums and possibly two tambourines, must have sounded like. In fact I can't remember ever hearing anything played by massed concertinas.

Anyway, they all look as if they are capable of putting on a jolly rousing performance. I just hope that the gentleman fourth from left on the back row, who has been a bit ambitious with his false whiskers, did not get them caught up in his concertina.

Salvation Army Concertina Band

Pinstone Street, around 1925

The major change in the appearance of Pinstone Street, seen here in the 1920s, has been the disappearance of St Paul's Church which stood on the site of what is now St Paul's Gardens (commonly called the Peace Gardens).

The church closed in 1937 and the site was bought by the Corporation. There was talk of building a cinema, shops or offices but the choice was eventually gardens, which were opened to the public in 1939.

Meanwhile a new St Paul's Church — a replica of the Pinstone Street building — was built at Arbourthorne. Now that too has gone. It was demolished in 1976.

The shops have changed too, of course. Bloom's Ltd, the opticians and photographic suppliers, can be seen on the right of the picture, at the corner of Charles Street. Coming down the other side of Pinstone Street, the shops are Stewart and Stewart Ltd, William Wreghitt, hatter, Foggitt's Health Food Stores, Southall and Co, boot and shoe dealers, Madam Baker Ltd, blouse specialists, Ernest G. Stauber, chocolate manufacturer ('Chocolate Expert', as it says above the shop), and a little bit of Alexandre's, tailors, can be seen at the edge of the picture.

St Paul's Church

ROYAL VISIT TO SHEFFIELD OF
H.R.H. THE PRINCE OF WALES. MAY 29TH 1923
GRAND HOTEL EMPLOYEES IN ATTENDANCE
F. STOKES.   J. PILLEY   P. JULES.
E. MABILLARD   A. CURCHOD   R. ORIO.
(MAITRE D'HOTEL)

Royal visit to Sheffield, 1923

His Majesty The King presenting new Colours. To The K.O.Y.L.I. in Weston Park, Sheffield 12.7.1905.

The Prince of Wales, who later became King Edward VIII, and later still became Duke of Windsor, visited Sheffield on 29 May, 1923 to open the new Town Hall extensions which included a library and conference room for councillors, a glass-domed rating hall, 39 new offices, seven strong rooms, an engine room, and five store rooms.

He also visited the university and went round three factories. He is somewhere on his way between these various engagements in the picture far left, watched by a large number of gentlemen — and one small boy — in flat caps.

The six impeccably turned out chaps, near left, are employees of the Grand Hotel who attended the Prince during his visit, by name Messrs F. Stokes, J. Pilley and P. Jules, standing, and Messrs E. Mabillard, A. Curchod (maître d'hotel) and R. Orio, seated. The only one I know anything about is Mr Orio, who left the Grand in 1938 to become proprietor of the Snake Inn.

The panoramic view above shows Weston Park on 12 July, 1905 when King Edward VII presented new colours to the King's Own Yorkshire Light Infantry. The gentry donned their silk hats and turned out in force that day, some of them watching proceedings from the roof of the Mappin Art Gallery.

Has it been raining, or has the path across the park been polished?

The stately homes of Sheffield — or some of them. All five were built more than 200 years ago, and three of them, Broom Hall, Beauchief Hall and Totley Hall, have survived. Walkley Hall, which stood near Heavygate Road, was demolished in the 1920s, and Lydgate Hall, seen here with croquet hoops on the lawn, and a tent up near the house, was demolished more recently.

Beauchief Hall, which has the date 1671 over the main door, was the home for many years of the Pegge-Burnell family, although after 1850, the family lived mostly at Winkburn, Notts, where they had another estate. In later years the hall became a private school, and it belongs now to De La Salle College.

Totley Hall has on it the date 1623. It was the home of the Coke family for some time, but its best remembered owner is probably Mr William Aldam Milner, magistrate, chairman of Ecclesall Guardians, Norton Rural Council and Totley parish council, and a member of Derbyshire County Council. Mr Milner died in 1931 and Sheffield Corporation bought the hall.

Broom Hall, once the home of the Jessop family, and of the Rev James Wilkinson, vicar of Sheffield for more than 50 years, no longer has the vast area of land that once went with it. In its time it has been turned into flats and offices. Now carefully restored, it is the only one of the five halls pictured here still in use as a private house.

Totley Hall

2276

Lydgate Hall

Laying of St Oswald's Foundation Stone mas.3

The lady laying the foundation stone of St Oswald's Church, Millhouses, is Mrs Firth, the wife of Mr Thomas Firth, who gave the site for the church. The date is 22 March, 1909. The building was dedicated in 1910, and consecrated in 1914. Because it had been built so near to the ancient boundary between Mercia and Northumbria, it was dedicated to King Oswald, the man who restored the Christian religion to Northumbria.

Norfolk Street Wesleyan Chapel, opposite, built in 1780, stood on the site of what is now the Victoria Hall. The end of Chapel Walk can be seen on the left of the picture. The chapel was demolished in 1906.

When the Wesleyan Chapel at Gleadless was photographed, below, it was still way out in the country. Now, the whole of the area around it is covered by housing estates.

Wesleyan Chapel, Gleadless

Norfolk Street Wesleyan Chapel

Darnall Church — Holy Trinity — has gone now. It v
demolished a few years ago and replaced by a sm
building. Much less lamented, the gentlemen's
convenience, by the gas lamp in the foreground, ha
gone too. It was not one of Darnall's outstanding
attractions.

The vicarage, in Industry Road, had a chequered
history. In the 18th century, it was a farm house. T
it became the home of Mr John Gaunt, a well-know
local benefactor, and when he died he left it to the
Church Commissioners. It was used as a vicarage
many years until a new vicarage was built in Mathe
Road, after which the old building served for a time
a mosque before being demolished.

According to legend it was once the home of Wi
Walker, who is reputed to have been the execution
King Charles I. It is also said that Charles Peace, or
Sheffield's more notorious citizens, who lived at
Darnall, once worked at the vicarage but was sack
by the vicar for stealing a clock. I cannot vouch for
either story.

The vicar, who can be seen with his family at the
entrance to the building, is the Rev George Gleada
Swann. He became curate of Darnall in 1888, and v
vicar from 1891 till 1912, when he moved to Pitsm

Darnall Vicarage

As an occasional patron of Darnall Cinema (also known, very appropriately, as the Little Cinema), an habitué of High Hazels Park during school holidays, and a train spotter at the nearby loco sheds, I used to know Darnall quite well. It has changed a great deal since I knew it, and even more since these pictures were taken.

Up to 1909 (when the tram service was extended outwards to Finchwell Road, Handsworth) Main Road, Darnall, used to be the end of the line. Trams reversed at Main Road ready to go back to town. This was Darnall Terminus.

The word Terminus, however, was enlarged over the years so that it came to mean not just the bit of track where the trams turned round, but the whole area around the Staniforth Road-Main Road junction. My grandmother, for example, did her shopping in the area, but she never spoke of going to Darnall. She always said she was going to 'The Terminus', by which she meant any of the shops within a 250-yard radius of the actual tram terminus.

The man whose name appears on the Main Road photograph — Mr A. Parish — had a shop close by the tram terminus. My abiding recollection of his shop is going there in 1945 to buy the first fireworks I ever bought.

Having been deprived of fireworks for the previous six years (explosive materials were needed for other things at the time) there was great excitement when word went round that Parish's had some in. I seem to remember that they were in such demand that each customer was only allowed to buy a certain number.

Darnall Terminus

FROM FORGE DAM, SHEFFIELD

Fulwood

One of the advantages of being a journalist on a morning newspaper is that you do not have to go to work until after lunch. By way of relaxation, some years ago, two or three of us used to spend the occasional summer morning knocking golf balls around the nine-hole pitch and putt course at Bingham Park, or Royal and Ancient Bingham, as we used to call it.

If memory serves me, the photograph opposite must have been taken about halfway down the fairway of the seventh, no more than a short chip and a little dribble from the hole. Being left handed at golf, I have sliced one or two down to the bottom of this hill in my time. The greenhouses were never in any danger though. I couldn't hit that far.

After a good solid tee shot had gone roughly where it was intended, I used to quite enjoy this view across Endcliffe and Ranmoor. But on occasions when I sliced, and the ball squirted off downhill to the hedge bottom, the view lost some of its enchantment.

A bit higher up the same valley, there are some very good views to be had of Fulwood, with Fulwood Church on the skyline, lots of trees, and Forge Dam boating pool at the bottom of the hill.

We were not too enthusiastic about boating, though. Pitch and putt was more our game.

CLIFFE AND RANMOOR.
OM BINGHAM PARK, SHEFFIELD. 2665,

Endcliffe and Ranmoor

Sheffield used to get quite a lot of visits from foreign potentates and dignitaries. The Shah of Persia called on one occasion. So did Crown Prince Rudolf of Austria, King Lewanika of Barotseland, the King of Portugal, Admiral Togo, The Emperor of Brazil, General Grant, Prince Carol of Rumania and the King of Uganda, to mention only a few.

What they usually did was call in on the Lord Mayor, trot round two or three steelworks, and then have a spot of dinner somewhere, often at the Cutlers' Hall.

The gentlemen above, pictured outside the Royal Victoria Hotel, are a party of Basuto chiefs who visited Sheffield and did all the usual things on 24 February, 1909. I see one of them brought his umbrella with him. He was probably well advised.

The scene opposite is not a still from an old Busby Berkeley movie, although it would not be too difficult to imagine Dick Powell popping up somewhere with a song and tout ensemble going into a vigorous tap routine.

In fact it is the cast of Sheffield Pageant of Production, a spectacular written by L. du Garde Peach and staged at the City Hall in November, 1948. Simultaneously, an exhibition called 'Sheffield on its Mettle' was held at the Cutlers' Hall after being opened by Princess Margaret on 15 November.

The pageant was quite something. It featured 126 singers from three large choirs, 56 dancers from nine dancing schools, seven parade girls, 96 crowd actors and 44 others who were described in the programme as 'isotypes'.

It was intended to dispel post-war gloom, to stir up local pride and give the city a dash of colour and some enjoyment. In the process, it probably made fuller use of the City Hall stage than any other presentation before or since.

Sheffield on its Mettle, 1948

The Sheffield and District Railway Servants Privilege Ticket Committee, 1905

The railway line, opposite, at Dore and Totley Station (as it used to be called) looks a mess after what happened on 9 October, 1907.

The 1.30 pm express from Sheffield to Birmingham and Bristol, pulled by two locomotives, was passing Dore Junction when the second engine ran foul of the points and plunged off the rails. The train ran on for 120 yards, and as it slowed, the derailed second engine crashed on to its side hitting the station platform and smashing off its dome. The driver and fireman were thrown out of the cab, and although they were cut and bruised escaped serious injury. Several coaches were also derailed but they stayed upright and there were no injuries among the large number of passengers.

At the time the crash happened — 1.42 pm — a north-bound express from Nottingham to Sheffield was due to pass through Dore, and the overturned engine, although not obstructing the down line itself, had ripped up a rail which was now in the path of the Nottingham train. The local signalman immediately changed the down signals to danger, and the fireman of the pilot engine ran along the line and placed fog signals in the track of the Nottingham train which came to a halt within 250 yards of the wreckage.

The line was blocked for several days.

Under headlines saying 'Sheffield Train's Marvellous Escape. Double Disaster Narrowly Averted. Locomotive Overturned at Dore', the next day's newspapers rejoiced in three fortunate aspects of the incident: first, that the crew of the derailed engine were not trapped in its fall; second, that the coaches of the train had stayed upright and coupled together; and third, that the Nottingham express had been prevented from running into the wreckage.

The upper postcard, left, was produced by a man called Mr Warner Gothard, of Barnsley. It shows the people and trains involved when a Liverpool to Grimsby emigrant train with 300 passengers crashed into the rear of a mineral train at Woodhouse Junction on 29 February, 1908. The guard of the goods train was killed immediately, and a fireman died of his injuries the following day.

Mr Gothard specialised in photographic montage cards of this kind, showing royal visits, notable events, and, quite often, disasters. He contrived to get a surprising number of photographs and a great deal of information on to a 5½-inch by 3½-inch postcard, and nowadays these cards are eagerly sought by collectors.

I'm unsure of the precise nature of the duties of the Sheffield and District Railway Servants Privilege Ticket Committee, but whatever they did, this is them, in 1905.

Disaster at Dore & Totley Station, 1907

Twitchells and leppings.

For those who are not familiar with the word, twitchells are small, narrow paths, the rural equivalent of gennels, or jinnels.

Seen left is a fine example of the genre at High Wincobank, or Shiregreen as it is now called. These particular twitchells were a short cut between High Wincobank and Low Wincobank, which is probably how the track came to be so well worn, short cuts being very popular.

Leppings, for those who are unfamiliar with this word too, are stepping stones across a river or stream. Sheffield's most famous leppings are those opposite, because they were near a street which stills bears their name today — Leppings Lane.

Although this postcard was published in the early 1900s, the actual photograph was taken much earlier, probably some time in the 1880s, and it shows that the stones, even though they are well worn, are very big. Only pedestrians used the stones, of course; carts were driven through the water. It is possible to see the cart tracks on either side of the river to the left of the stones. I don't think the young man standing on one of the stones has any intention of crossing. I think he is idling time away throwing a few skimmers across the water.

The Twitchells, High Wincobank

Piper Lane, Pitsmoor

Leppings Lane in the 1880's

New Church Street is difficult to visualise. It ran between Norfolk Street and Pinstone Street through the site of what is now the Town Hall. So this view, looking towards Pinstone Street, must have been taken in the early 1890s, before demolition work started for the Town Hall.

The street seems to have been very well provided with public houses. The Cutlers' Arms, at number 7, was obviously still in business when the picture was taken. There are two men, a woman and a dog in the doorway. The Green Man, kept by Benjamin Wardle, at number 9, looks as though it is still in use. But The Grapes, at number 11, looks deserted. The door is closed, there are no curtains, and the sign has been removed. It may be that The Grapes was the first building to be vacated for demolition.

The picture of Broad Street, Park, is not the Broad Street we know today. The bit of street at the extreme right of the picture is Dixon Lane, with the Norfolk Arms on the corner with Shude Hill.

Mount Zion sounds, and even looks, a bit like a church. But it was a private house and its real name was Wesley Tower, Lydgate Lane. When it was offered for sale in 1913, it was said to have 'a lofty tower from which extensive views of the country around Sheffield can be seen'.

The very old picture of Bishop's House is the only photograph I have ever seen taken in Sheffield which includes a man wearing a yokel-type smock.

Broad St Park. JWM

Bishops Cottage. Sheffield. JW

Mount Zion

70

Mount Zion

Bishop's Cottage

Hendon St.

G.Sprigg.
Handsworth.

Handsworth and Woodhouse, before they came into Sheffield in 1921, were joined together under one urban district council, although there was always a certain amount of rivalry between the two. As one who was brought up in Handsworth and educated at Woodhouse, I had a foot in both camps.

Being absorbed by Sheffield brought about a number of changes, one of which was that Henry Street, Handsworth, where the Co-op was, was renamed Hendon Street.

Retford Road, once called Worksop Road, is exactly as I remember it as a child. Nowadays, most of the trees have gone and it has become a dual carriageway, with all that that implies.

The postcard showing The Stag, one of Woodhouse's many public houses, seems to have been issued as a form of advertisement. On the reverse it says that the builder was John Middleton, of Bridge Street, Sheffield, and the architects were Messrs. Gibbs, Flockton and Teather, of St. James Row, Sheffield.

Retford Rd Handsworth.   3144.

Retford Road, Handsworth

The Stag, Woodhouse

Having mentioned Handsworth Co-op, I thought, to prevent any accusations of favouritism, that I had better mention Woodhouse Co-op. This is it below, with three, or possibly three and a half, members of staff in their spotless white overalls and aprons, posing outside, and a nice line in net curtains in the left hand window. There are not many customers about, but perhaps it was early in the day and they had only just opened.

Two features stand out in the picture of Garden Walk, below left. One is the little girl, carrying a basket or container of some kind. If she had a hat on she would look like Little Red Riding Hood on her way to her grandma's. The other is the splendid selection of stiles and gates.

Beighton Road, Woodhouse, seen here about 1914, looks exactly the same as when I used to walk along it in the 1950s. I suppose the shopkeepers must have changed, but everything else looks the same. I cannot remember where I found this card, but it was sent to a friend by a lady called Hardcastle, which is a well known Woodhouse name. There have been Hardcastles in the village for at least 200 years.

arden Walk, Woodhouse

Woodhouse Co-op

Furnace Lane, Woodhouse Mill

The odd thing about the children at the bottom of Furnace Lane, Woodhouse Mill, above, is that six of them have their hands to their mouths, which means, I suppose, that they are either eating or sucking their fingers. The picture was taken about 1914.

I used to know this bit of Furnace Lane quite well. The shop with the sun blind on the left used to sell very good bottles of pop which I sampled occasionally, and another shop on the other side of Retford Road (the houses in the middle distance are on Retford Road) sold a form of triangular ice tube called a Joystick, which was ambrosia to a hungry schoolboy. I can almost taste one just by typing the name.

Beighton is one of the more recent additions to Sheffield. It became part of the city — somewhat reluctantly — in the boundary extensions of April, 1967.

When the pictures opposite were taken, around the time of the First World War, it was still a small Derbyshire village well outside Sheffield. The Rother used to overflow occasionally and cause a bit of flooding, but otherwise life must have been very peaceful and agreeable.

Beighton

VE ARCHES *

A Great Central 4-6-0 hauls a line of non-corridor coaches across the five arches at Hillsborough, with only one building in view. In the foreground is a large area of grassland called Rawson's Meadows, from the Rawson family who owned land in this area for many years.

The route through the arches, which was only a footpath at the time the picture was taken, was transformed in later years by the building of Herries Road and although the arches are still there, the railway has declined in importance and the meadows are long gone. The name Rawson lives on in the names of a number of surrounding streets.